Growing A Healthy
Community

This book has been provided by

**Carlisle Area Health and
Wellness Foundation**

*to support improved health and wellness
in our communities.*

Reducing and Recycling Waste

Carol Inskipp

GARETH**STEVENS**
PUBLISHING
A World Almanac Education Group Company

Please visit our web site at: www.garethstevens.com
For a free color catalog describing Gareth Stevens Publishing's list of high-quality books and multimedia programs, call 1-800-542-2595 (USA) or 1-800-387-3178 (Canada). Gareth Stevens Publishing's fax: (414) 332-3567.

Library of Congress Cataloging-in-Publication Data

Inskipp, Carol.
    Reducing and recycling waste / Carol Inskipp.
      p. cm. — (Improving our environment)
    Includes bibliographical references and index.
    ISBN 0-8368-4429-7 (lib. bdg.)
    Contents: Drowning in waste — The mess we make — Toxic waste — What happens to trash? — The three Rs of garbage — What can we recycle? — Working glass — Plastic planet — Saving paper — Aluminum recycling — Making compost — Reuse — Get involved!
    1. Refuse and refuse disposal—Juvenile literature. 2. Recycling (Waste, etc.)—Juvenile literature.
I. Title. II. Series.
TD792.I57   2005
363.72'8—dc22
                                                        2004056597

This North American edition first published in 2005 by
Gareth Stevens Publishing
A World Almanac Education Group Company
330 West Olive Street, Suite 100
Milwaukee, WI 53212 USA

This U.S. edition copyright © 2005 by Gareth Stevens, Inc. Original edition copyright © 2005 by Hodder Wayland. First published in 2005 by Hodder Wayland, an imprint of Hodder Children's Books, a division of Hodder Headline Limited, 338 Euston Road, London NW1 3BH, U.K.

Series Editor: Victoria Brooker
Editor: Margot Richardson
Designer: Fiona Webb
Artwork: Peter Bull
Gareth Stevens Editor: Carol Ryback
Gareth Stevens Designer: Steve Schraenkler

Photo credits: Chapel Studios/Zul Mukhida title page, 27. Ecoscene Photo Library: Jan Bower 11; Phillip Colla 19; Vicki Coombs 29. Laurel Firestone 13. FPLA: G. Marcoaldi/©Panda Photo 15; S. & D. & K. Maslowski 24; Mike J. Thomas 25. Still Pictures: Thomas Rapauch 4; Jeff Greenberg 5; Martin Wyness 8; J. P. Sylvestre 9; Dylan Garcia 12, 16; Hartmut Schwarzbach 17; John Cancalosi 18; Andre Maslenmnikov 20, 21; Mark Edwards 22; Ray Pfortner 23; Argus 26. Topham Picturepoint: 6; Tony Savino/Image Works 7. Hodder Wayland Photo Library: Angela Hampton 28.

Printed in China

1 2 3 4 5 6 7 8 9 09 08 07 06 05

Contents

Words in **bold** can be found in the glossary.

Drowning in Waste

Every day, people discard leftover food, glass, cans, plastic, newspapers, junk mail, and old clothes. We also throw out large items, such as refrigerators, cars, and computers. Factories and industries create solid and liquid wastes, and the natural gas, oil, and coal we burn for power produces even more waste.

All over the world, people are buying more and more goods and throwing out increasing amounts of garbage. As the world **population** increases, greater numbers of people add to growing mountains of trash.

Landfills are quickly filling with our garbage. ▼

A lot of our garbage comes from packaging wrapped around the stuff we buy. Many products are single-use items. If, say, a washing machine breaks down, its owner might just throw it out instead of repairing it. Cell phones that break down usually end up on the scrap heap. Factories, mines, and power plants also create waste products when they manufacture and process goods, dig for metal ores, or produce energy.

◄ **Household waste contains different types of refuse, including paper, aluminum cans, and plastic.**

TRY THIS! **What Type of Waste?**

Make a waste chart for your home and hang it on the wall above the garbage can. Ask everyone to list whatever is thrown away for a week: food waste, clothing, newspapers, cardboard, glass bottles, plastic, packaging materials, cans — whatever. Count the totals when the week is over. What takes up the most space? What could be **reused** instead?

KNOW THE FACTS

In 2001, the average American citizen created twice as much trash as someone in Europe and nearly seven times as much garbage as a person from India.

The Mess We Make

Our garbage threatens Earth and all life on it. Waste also dirties our **atmosphere**.

Dumped or burned rubbish causes water and air **pollution** that is harmful to people, wildlife, and the **environment**. Factory and mining **by-products** also cause pollution if they are not disposed of properly.

Home and factory waste flows into a canal in a Chinese city. ▼

Using Up Resources

Making and using new goods uses up the world's valuable **natural resources** (living and nonliving materials that occur naturally and are useful to us, such as **fossil fuels**). If we continue using our natural resources at present rates, we will leave almost nothing for future **generations**.

Waste Gases

Carbon dioxide gas (CO_2), naturally present in the atmosphere, helps keep Earth warm enough for us to live comfortably. The burning of fossil fuels, such as oil, natural gas, or coal, produces waste CO_2 gas and adds to the CO_2 already in the atmosphere. As a result, the atmosphere traps more heat, which causes higher worldwide temperatures and makes storms more frequent and severe.

▲ Weather experts believe that **global warming** is causing an increasing number of violent storms and flooding. Storms often destroy many homes, as in this trailer park in Barefoot Bay, Florida.

7

Toxic Waste

Much of our waste contains chemicals that are **toxic**, or poisonous. If not used carefully or disposed of safely, toxic materials may damage our health or the environment.

A number of products that we use every day in our homes, from paints, cleaners, oils, **pesticides**, and air fresheners to computers, smoke detectors, and televisions, contain toxic chemicals. Factories and industries also produce toxics.

◄ Computers contain some toxic materials. These poisons find their way into the air, soil, and water supply when computers are discarded.

Where Does It Go?

People know very little about who produces toxic waste, how much is produced, or where it goes. When released into the environment, toxic chemicals travel freely in the air, get into rivers, and find their way into the oceans. Wildlife and humans breathe in these poisons, absorb them through their skin, or eat or drink them with food and liquids. New research shows that even very low levels of poisons can kill plants and damage the health of people and animals and can sometimes cause diseases such as cancer.

▲ Beluga whales from the St. Lawrence River between the United States and Canada are so highly poisoned by chemicals that their bodies are considered toxic waste when they die.

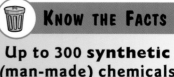 **KNOW THE FACTS**

Up to 300 **synthetic (man-made) chemicals** have been found in humans. Even babies have synthetic chemicals in their bodies that were passed to them from their mothers.

What Happens to Trash?

People dispose of garbage in different ways. They bury it, burn it, dump it in the ocean, reuse it, or make it into new, usable items.

Landfill Sites

Many countries either bury trash in big holes or use it to build a "waste mountain." Food and garden waste rots away (decomposes) quickly. Other garbage, such as plastic, may take hundreds of years to decompose — or it may never decompose. As the waste pile breaks down, it often releases toxic chemicals to the air, soil, and groundwater. **Methane**, a **greenhouse gas** that helps cause global warming, is also emitted. Noise, nasty smells, dust, and litter can create problems for people who live near landfill sites.

Garbage decomposes at various rates. ▼

Glass bottle - NEVER

Disposable diaper - 500 years

Plastic bottle - 450 years

Aluminum can - 300 years

Steel can - 100 years

Wool clothing - 1 year

Paper bag - 1 month

Burning

Sometimes the energy produced by burning waste is used to make electricity, but the smoke may cause serious air pollution. Researchers believe that burning garbage produces many of the gases that help cause global warming.

Dumping at Sea

Some wastes dumped in the oceans contain toxics that poison sea life.

Recycling and Reuse

Recycling means either making the waste product into the same item — such as melting cans to make new cans — or producing a completely new product, such as making fencing from plastic bottles. When things are reused, they are cleaned and used again in their original form instead of being remade.

▲ Many countries burn their waste. This plant in Hong Kong houses an incinerator (a huge oven for burning materials such as waste).

The Three Rs of Garbage

You can help cut waste by practicing
the three Rs of garbage: reduce, reuse
and recycle.

Reduce

Everyone can help reduce waste at home by simply buying
and using less of everything. Share or borrow rather than
purchasing new products. Look for food and merchandise
with less packaging whenever possible. Take your own cloth
bags to grocery stores to avoid using their plastic bags.

Food packaging creates large amounts of waste. Choose foods with less packaging to help reduce your waste. ▼

Reuse

Many useful objects get thrown out every day. Sheets of paper with writing on only one side could be used as scrap paper for quick notes. Some **disposable** plastic cups and food containers are reusable after washing and rinsing. Repair shops, family members, or friends can fix broken tools, sporting goods, or appliances. Dry cleaners can mend torn clothes, and a shoe repair shop can resole shoes.

Recycle

It often takes less energy to make new goods from recycled materials, and it uses fewer natural resources than making merchandise from scratch. Some recycled products, such as plastic boards, may last longer than the real thing.

HELPING OUT

Promote recycling at your school with an art contest. Ask students to use as many recycled materials as possible to create their sculptures, paintings, and fabric art.

What Can We Recycle?

Many of the items that normally get thrown in the trash can be recycled instead.

How Does Recycling Work?

Many people collect recyclable materials and take them to recycling centers for cash. Some communities provide residents with recycling carts that are emptied the same day as garbage pick-up day. Recyclable materials are sorted, cleaned, and made into new products.

Remaking the Same Products

Many materials, such as **aluminum** cans, steel cans, glass bottles, and newspapers, are remade into the same products.

You can recycle many items instead of throwing them away. ▼

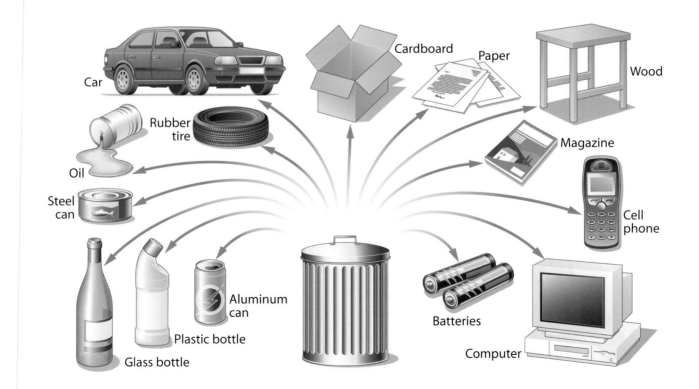

Car

Rubber tire

Oil

Steel can

Glass bottle

Plastic bottle

Aluminum can

Cardboard

Paper

Wood

Magazine

Cell phone

Batteries

Computer

14

Totally New Products

Some recycling processes turn trash into completely different products. Recycled plastics are made into fleece clothing. Tires are remade into crash barriers, road materials, floor mats, and even shoes. Some countries burn tires for energy, but that practice pollutes the environment.

▲ Warm fleece clothing is made from recycled plastic. About five recycled drink bottles make enough fiber for one fleece jacket.

TRY THIS!

Recycling List

Find at least ten newspaper or magazine pictures of items that are often thrown away, such as soft drink bottles, books, clothing, paint, cars, furniture, and toys. Make a list of the raw materials used to create these products. Could any of the materials in your pictures be reused or recycled? How?

Working Glass

Glass does not decompose like most trash put into a landfill. But it can be recycled many times without any loss of quality.

Glass is made from a mixture of sand, limestone, a chemical called sodium carbonate, and other materials that are heated to very high temperatures. Glass is ideal packaging for food and drinks because it preserves the taste and freshness of its contents without affecting the flavor.

People in many countries clean and recycle used glass bottles for soft drinks. ▼

Advantages of Recycling Glass

Glass recycling is one of the first steps in saving the environment. The practice of recycling glass products includes the following advantages:

- Lowers waste-disposal costs
- Keeps glass out of landfills
- Decreases use of **raw materials**
- Saves energy. (It takes about 25 percent less energy to recycle glass than to make new glass.)
- Cuts air **pollutants** produced by glassmaking from raw materials by more than 20 percent
- Helps raise awareness of waste disposal problems

▲ Used glass is broken into small pieces at a glass recycling factory. Workers watch for paper labels or metal caps and remove them before the glass is melted down.

KNOW THE FACTS

A recycled glass bottle saves enough energy to run a 100-watt lightbulb for four hours. Most bottles and jars made in the United States contain some recycled glass.

17

Plastic Planet

All plastics are oil-based products. The production of plastics causes pollution. Most plastics take hundreds of years to decompose.

Toxic Plastic

Plastic litters every corner of the world. It even washes up on remote islands where nobody lives and people seldom visit. Plastic refuse strangles wildlife, blocks drains, and litters riverbanks. Discarded plastic takes up space in landfills. Almost all plastic requires a very long time to break down, if it can break down; some plastics last virtually forever. As plastic decomposes, toxic **particles** pollute soil and water. The burning of waste plastic emits (gives off) poisonous gases.

Every year, plastic bags ▶ kill an estimated one hundred thousand seabirds, whales, seals, and turtles in oceans around the world. This wild stork in Spain cannot eat because it is trapped in a plastic bag.

▲ Four million plastic detergent bottles were recycled into **plastic lumber** to provide a new boardwalk and viewing system around the Old Faithful Geyser in Yellowstone National Park in Wyoming.

Recycling

Plastic comes in many different forms, so recycling plastics is more complicated than recycling glass, metals, or paper. In the United States, each type of plastic is labeled because each needs a different treatment in the recycling process.

TRY THIS!

Compare Packaging

Collect six types of plastic packaging. Make a list of packaging materials that could substitute for the plastic, such as cardboard or paper. Compare your new packaging ideas to the existing packaging. Are yours environmentally friendly?

KNOW THE FACTS

The U.S. recycles about 18 percent of its plastic containers and about 36 percent of its soft drink bottles. This saves enough energy to power a city the size of Atlanta, Georgia, for one year. Still, lots of waste plastic ends up in landfills.

Saving Paper

Paper plays a large part in our lives, but papermaking uses huge amounts of chemicals, energy, and water and creates much air and water pollution.

Less than one-fifth of the world's population (people living in the United States, Europe, and Japan) use nearly three-quarters of the world's paper. By 2010, the level of paper use around the globe is expected to increase by one-half.

Losing Forests

Cutting trees for papermaking helps destroy Earth's forests. More than 40 percent of the cut trees become some type of paper. Every year, we use up an area of natural forest one-half the size of England. This rate of forest loss is **unsustainable** because the forests are not being replaced.

A sustainable logging plan includes planting one tree for every tree cut and removed from the forest. ▼

Paper and the Three Rs

Reducing paper use and reusing or recycling paper helps lessen the harmful environmental effects resulting from paper production and use. Compared to other materials, paper is easy to recycle. Almost any type of paper, including used newspapers, cardboard, packaging, stationery, junk mail, and wrapping paper, can be recycled. But there is a limit. After being recycled about five to seven times, paper fibers shorten too much to make useful paper.

◄ Old paper is shredded into small pieces during the recycling process. The paper pieces are then mixed with water and made into pulp. New paper is made from the pulp.

HELPING OUT

Poster Power

Design a poster to persuade students in your school to reuse and recycle paper.

Aluminum Recycling

Producing aluminum from raw materials
is expensive, but recycling it is economical.
Recycling doesn't affect the quality of
aluminum, so it can be recycled forever.

Aluminum comes from bauxite ore. It takes huge amounts of electricity to separate the pure aluminum metal, called alumina, from the rest of the ore. Large quantities of pollutants, including contaminated muds and waste carbon dioxide (CO_2) gas, are also produced. In countries without strict controls, the mining and **smelting** of aluminum causes much environmental damage.

Removing one ton (0.99 tonne) of aluminum from bauxite ore produces about 794 pounds (360 kilograms) of solid wastes and 1.6 tons (1.5 tonnes) of a watery, lumpy mud, called slurry. Iron in the bauxite ore causes the red color. ▼

▲ Recycling companies make money from the waste materials they collect. Aluminum cans for recycling are worth about five times more than glass or plastic bottles.

Recycling Aluminum Cans

Aluminum drink cans are the most cost-effective containers to recycle. Making aluminum cans from recycled aluminum saves nearly 95 percent of the energy used to produce cans from scratch. Aluminum recycling also produces 95 percent less air and water pollution than making aluminum from ore. Brazil leads the world in aluminum can recycling. In 2002, Brazilians recycled 87 percent of their aluminum cans.

KNOW THE FACTS

In 2002, more than half of the United States's aluminum cans were recycled, making them the most recycled item in the U.S. If you could stack the U.S. aluminum cans that are not recycled, they would reach the moon in just five weeks!

Making Compost

Food and yard wastes make up more than one-third of all household garbage. Most of this kind of waste makes good **compost** for growing flowers and more food.

Kitchen and garden rubbish, called **organic waste**, produces good material for enriching a garden, but wild animals also like to dig through it. Some people carefully stir their backyard compost heaps to bury and mix in the new wastes and help them decompose faster. Organic waste in landfills breaks down more gradually than in a garden compost heap.

Household wastes often attract pests. These raccoons in Ohio raid a trash can for some tasty snacks. ▼

The best way to make compost is by mixing layers of food waste, backyard waste, and garden soil. After about three months, it all rots into a crumbly, earthy mixture. People with small yards or who live in apartments could use a large plastic composting bin. Other people set up a worm tank, where worms eat their way through garbage rather quickly.

▲ A backyard compost heap reduces the amount of garbage that ends up in landfill sites. Material from a compost heap not only helps flowers grow but also helps keep landfills from filling up.

TRY THIS! ## See How Compost is Made

- Place 2 inches (5 centimeters) of damp soil in the bottom of a clear container.
- Place 2-inch (5-cm) layers of food, leaf, and grass scraps on top of the soil.
- Repeat the layers of soil, food, leaf, and grass scraps.
- Leave the container open and place it on a windowsill.
- Add a little water every week and stir the contents to keep them moist.
- Take notes on how the material changes over a three-month time period.

Reuse

Reusing things whenever possible is an even better way to help save the environment than recycling them.

Although recycling is a good way to reduce waste and save natural resources and energy, the process requires added energy and raw materials. In contrast, reused items remain in their original form. No new raw materials or much extra energy are necessary in order to simply reuse objects.

Computer companies hope to develop new uses for old computer parts. ▼

Ways to Reuse

There are many opportunities for reusing things. People in Denmark, for instance, use refillable plastic bottles for milk and soft drinks. Customers drink the contents and bring the containers back to the stores for refilling. Increasingly, computer companies accept used equipment and reuse some of the computer parts to upgrade older computers and resell them.

Developed countries could learn much from **developing countries**, where higher proportions of waste are reused or recycled. People in some areas make soles for shoes from tires. Cups and jugs are often made from tin cans.

◀ This Kenyan woman makes money by repairing secondhand shoes. She buys old shoes, fixes them, and then sells them.

Get Involved!

Always remember the three Rs of waste: reduce, reuse, recycle. Each of these actions improves the environment.

Reduce

You can reduce waste by thinking about what you throw away. Do you really need to discard that item? The best way to reduce waste is to buy only things you really need. Buying quality goods that will last a long time helps cut waste and preserves our natural resources.

We can help cut waste and improve our environment by carefully choosing the goods we buy. ▼

Reuse

Reuse containers whenever possible. Refill printer ink cartridges instead of buying new ones. Hang a bird feeder from a tree using an old dog leash. Store extra screws or nails in old food jars. Save egg cartons, plastic food containers, and popsicle sticks for arts and crafts projects. Use plastic grocery bags to line household garbage cans. Cut winter drafts by taping bubble wrap from packaging to windows. Give unwanted clothes, books, and toys to charities, churches, or shelters for the homeless.

Recycle

As well as reusing things, make a point to recycle more at home and at school. Buy recycled products, too. If your school doesn't have a recycling center, ask your teachers how to establish one. Make compost from kitchen, garden, and yard waste.

▲ **One person's trash is another person's treasure. Look for bargains at rummage sales.**

Glossary

aluminum a strong, light, silvery-gray metal that does not corrode easily.

atmosphere the layers of gases that surround and protect Earth.

by-products second, less important but very useful products made from the leftovers of a main product.

carbon dioxide a gas that is naturally present in the atmosphere but is also produced as a waste gas when anything is burned and when living organisms breathe.

compost leftover food scraps and garden waste that decays to produce a rich fertilizer for growing plants and flowers.

developed country a rich country with well-developed industries.

developing countries poorer countries with fewer or less-developed industries.

disposable made to be discarded after one use.

environment the physical conditions of the areas where people, animals, or plants live.

fossil fuels fuels, such as coal, oil, and natural gas, that formed from the fossilized remains of plants and animals.

generations groups of people, all roughly the same age, who grow up together in time periods that follow one another, such as grandparents, parents, and children.

global warming the worldwide rise in average annual temperatures caused by pollution and some natural disasters.

greenhouse gases the gases, such as carbon dioxide and methane, that contribute to global warming.

methane a colorless, odorless, flammable greenhouse gas produced by burning certain fuels and by the decay of organic waste.

natural resources living and nonliving materials, such as plants, oil, and limestone, used for food, fuel, or buildings.

organic waste plant or animal matter that eventually decays.

particles very tiny pieces.

pesticides substances that destroy insects or other pests.

plastic lumber recycled plastic shaped into boards and used in the same way as wood.

pollutant a substance that changes and harms the air, water, or land.

pollution the results of harmful substances that damage the environment.

population the number of people, plants, or animals that live in a certain area.

raw materials basic materials that are used in their natural form or changed into another form (often combined with other raw or used materials) to create new objects.

recycling changing wastes, such as aluminum cans, into reusable materials.

reused used again.

solid waste unneeded solid materials.

slurry a semiliquid, often lumpy mixture.

smelting extracting pure metal from ore using heat; also called refining.

sustainable able to renew itself at the current rate of use without danger of complete destruction or permanent damage.

synthetic made by people; not natural.

toxic poisonous.

unsustainable unable to renew itself at the current rate of use without danger of complete destruction or permanent damage.

Further Information

Books

Aluminum. Recycle, Reduce, Reuse, Rethink (series). Kate Walker (Smart Apple Media)

Danube: Cyanide Spill. Environmental Disasters (series). Nicol Bryon (World Almanac Library)

Earth-Friendly Crafts for Kids: 50 Awesome Things to Make With Recycled Stuff. Heather Smith with Joe Rhatigan (Lark)

Exxon Valdez: Oil Spill. Environmental Disasters (series). Nicol Bryon (World Almanac Library)

Love Canal: Pollution Crisis. Environmental Disasters (series). Nicol Bryon (World Almanac Library)

Recycling. Environment Starts Here! (series). Angela Royston (Hodder Wayland)

Global Pollution. Face the Facts (series). Paul Brown (Heinemann)

Waste Disposal. Earth Watch (series). Sally Morgan (Franklin Watts)

Where Does Rubbish Go? S. Tahta (Usborne Publishing Ltd.)

Worms Eat My Garbage: How to Set Up and Maintain a Worm Composting System. Mary Applehof (Flower Press)

Reducing and Recycling Waste Web Sites

Environmental Kids Club
www.epa.gov/kids/garbage.htm

Greenpeace
www.greenpeace.org

National Energy Education Development
www.need.org/infobooks.htm

Natural Resources Kids Page
www.metrokc.gov/dnr/kidsweb/index.htm

Reduce, Reuse, Recycle
www.worldalmanacforkids.com/explore/environment2.html

United States Environmental Protection Agency — Aluminum
www.epa.gov/epaoswer/non-hw/muncpl/alum.htm

Welcome to the Museum of Solid Waste
www.eia.doe.gov/kids/recycling/

Zero Waste America
www.zerowasteamerica.org

Index

Numbers in **bold** refer to illustrations.